Fruits OF THE Spirit

A Bible study based on
Galatians 5:22-23

Victoria Fletcher

All verses written throughout this study are taken from the King James version of the Bible unless noted otherwise.

The front cover and title page photo is used courtesy of SermonCentral.com

copyright © 2020 Victoria Fletcher
ISBN: 978-1-7340868-1-2

Hoot Books Publishing
owner, Victoria Fletcher
vfletcher56@gmail.com

Color Code for the Fruits of the Spirit

love

joy

peace

patience

kindness

goodness

faithfulness

gentleness

self-control

Throughout all the verses used, you will see the nine fruits of the Spirit words color coded like above. You can see how many times they are used. I chose nine verses for each "fruit". Hope you'll dig and find even more.

Hope you will enjoy learning about the character descriptors that were used in Galatians 5:22-23.

And may your lives be ever fruitful and abundant in the good deeds you will produce by following the commands of Jesus, our Lord and Savior.

Okay, let's get started.

FRUIT OF THE SPIRIT

love,
joy,
peace,
patience,
kindness,
goodness,
faithfulness,
gentleness,
and self-control

Galatians 5:22-23

Hello Reader,
I am so blessed you chose this study to read. I hope it will be inspirational in your walk with the Lord so that these "fruits" will be displayed in your life daily as you strive to live your life in the Spirit.

When I was doing a Bible study on-line, I was reminded of the fruits of the Spirit. It immediately took me back to when I taught the children's choir at my church. In one of our musicals, it had the song "Fruits of the Spirit." It was really fast and rattled off the nine fruits. I ended up writing the fruits on a posterboard. We started slowly saying them together. Each week, we sped up a little more. By performance time, they nailed it. Well, that was over a decade ago and that song still plays in my head every time I hear "fruits of the Spirit."

I hope after our study that these nine fruits will quickly roll off your tongue, too:
Love, joy, peace, patience, kindness, goodness, faithfulness, gentleness, and self-control.

If you like a challenge, here is a link to the song from our musical on You Tube. Good luck.
https://youtu.be/teirSPJzUAE

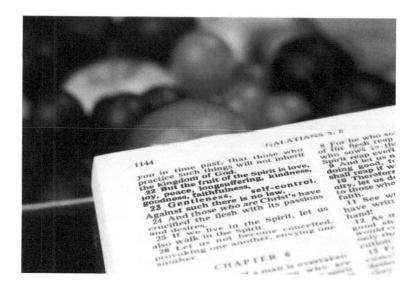

During this study, you can check the website page (fruitsofthespiritbiblestudy.com) and see the daily lessons, check out each post, leave comments, have discussions amongst yourselves, and post your daily activities.

In teaching Sunday School and the children's choir for 43 years at First Baptist Church in Damascus, Virginia, one of my favorite lessons/songs was about the fruits of the Spirit.

You will see nine verses for each fruit, a story to go with it, an activity to finish it up with, and a closing word or prayer. Hope you enjoy this journey with me as we learn how to be "fruitful" in God's world so that others see Him through us.

Love- A profoundly tender, passionate affection for another person.

Welcome to Day 1

Let's take a look at some verses that contain the word love. Even though I am writing them here, I encourage you to look them up in the Bible version that you most like to use. I like the King James version the best but also use the NIV, Holman, NSIB, and others when studying. Here we go:

John 3:16 *"For God so loved the world that He gave His only Begotten Son, that whosoever believeth in Him should not perish but have eternal life."*

1 John 4:7 *"Beloved, let us love one another: for love is of God; and everyone that loveth is born of God and knoweth God."*

1 John 4:19 *"We love Him because He first loved us."*

1 Corinthians 13:13 *"And now abideth faith, hope, charity (love), these three; but the greatest of these is charity (love)."*

John 15:12-13 *"This is my commandment, that ye love one another as I have loved you. Greater love hath no man than this, that a man lay down His life for his friends."*

1 John 4:8 *"He that loveth not knoweth not God; for God is love."*

Deuteronomy 6:5 *"And thou shalt love the LORD thy God with all thine heart and with all thy soul and with all thy might."*

Psalm 18:1 *"I will love Thee, O LORD, my strength."*

 **John 14:15** *"If ye love Me, keep My commandments."*

Let's talk about the greatest love there is and the gift He gave us. As you read in our very first verse, John 3:16, God's love—agape love— was given to us. He sent His only Son Jesus to come to earth to be our Sacrificial Lamb. God knows the sinful nature of us and knew we would need a Savior. He sent Jesus, who willingly died in our place. Wow!!! I think we should be in prayer every day thanking God and Jesus for loving us so much. If you haven't accepted Jesus as your Lord and Savior for coming to save you from your sins and give you eternal life with Him in heaven, I hope today is the day.

I accepted Jesus as my Savior during a revival at my church when I was only nine years old. I still sin every day of my life, but I know that I am saved by grace. I can go to the Lord in prayer and repent of my sins and know He hears me and forgives. I work harder to be obedient to the will of God so that when my time on earth is done, I can be in heaven with loved ones that have gone before me. What a great day of praise and rejoicing that will be. I want to be obedient to the commands God gave me to follow. I read and study my Bible daily and try to put into practice all the commands that He gives us.

I am looking forward to going through the rest of the fruits of the Spirit with you. Hope you plan to continue the trip with me.

Dear Father,

Thank you for the person reading this book. If they are not Your child, I hope they become one today. Let them know Your love and feel the Holy Spirit move in their life. Help me to say what You want me to say in this book so that others can come to know You. If they already do, I hope that they would grow in Your Word through this study. Thank You for Your love, mercy, grace, and forgiveness.

In Jesus' name I pray, Amen.

Before we leave each "fruit," I am adding a challenge activity for you to do. I would love to see you post these on our website.

The challenge activity for today is to take a verse of the Bible (preferably with love in it) and write it around the word LOVE.

Here's an example:

Be **L**oved, let us

l**O**ve one another, for

lo**V**e is of God and

Everyone that loveth God is born of God and
knoweth God.

Okay, it's your turn. Please remember to share on our website page (fruitsofthespiritbiblestudy.com).

L

O

V

E

For God
so lo**V**ed the world
that he g**A**ve
His on **L**y
b**E**gotten
so**N**
tha**T** whosoever
believeth **I**n Him
should **N**ot perish
but have **E**verlasting
life.

John 3:16

Joy

Joy- The emotion of great delight, a happiness caused by something exceptionally good or satisfying.

Welcome to Day 2

Let's look at our verses for the day that contain the word joy. Look them up in your Bible version and read them as well. I also encourage you to find more. You can list them on our website. Go to blog for Day 2- Joy.

 James 1:2-3 *"My brethren, count it all joy when you fall into divers (many) temptations; knowing this, that the trying of your faith worketh patience."*

 Romans 15:13 *"Now the God of Hope will fill you with all joy and peace in believing, that ye may abound in hope through the power of the Holy Ghost."*

 **Psalm 30:5** *"For His anger endureth but a moment; in His favor is life: weeping may endure for a night, but joy cometh in the morning."*

 **Hebrews 12:2** *"Looking unto Jesus, the author and finisher of our faith; who for the joy that was set before Him, endured the cross, despising the shame, and is set down at the right hand of the throne of God."*

 **1 Thessalonians 5:16-18** *"Rejoice evermore. Pray without ceasing. In everything give thanks: for this is the will of God in Christ Jesus concerning you."*

 Philippians 4:4 *"Rejoice in the Lord always: and again I say, Rejoice."*

 **Psalm 16:11** *"Thou wilt shew me the path of life: in Thy presence is fullness of joy; at Thy right hand there are pleasures forevermore."*

John 16:24 *"Hitherto have ye asked nothing in My name: ask, and ye shall receive, that your joy may be full."*

 **Luke 1:14** *"And thou shalt have joy and gladness; and many shall rejoice at his birth."* *(speaking of John the Baptist)*

When I was in Sunday School, my teacher said to know real joy, you had to

put **J**esus first in your life

then **O**thers should follow and

lastly, **Y**ou.

So many in our world today only know YO!!! They think of themselves above all else. We are in a pandemic at the time I am writing this battling the coronavirus or COVID-19. I wonder if it is God's way of getting the world's attention that He needs to be first in our lives. For some, that lesson has not been learned because they are hoarding supplies and not adhering to the rules to help stop this virus.

When we get through this time, I can only hope that some of them can come to know Jesus as their Lord and Savior before it is too late.

Okay, enough sadness on our day of JOY. Let's come up with things that bring you joy. Below is my example. You don't even have to limit it to the letters in JOY. I just love acrostics and couldn't resist. Be creative. Write a poem or song. Use other acrostic words. Be sure to share on our website. Go to blog for Day 2- Joy.

Jesus, jigsaw puzzles, just relaxing

Opening my Bible or another book to read

Yummy snacks, yakking with friends

As we close today, let's take time to say a prayer. Remember to tell God and Jesus how much you are thankful for the JOY they give us. I learned a way to help me in my prayer time. It uses the fingers on a hand to remember things we should pray for. The thumb is the closest, so you pray for those closest to you like family and friends. The index is the pointer, so you pray for teachers, doctors, anyone that guides you. The third finger is the top one, so you pray for our leaders. The ring finger is the weakest, so you pray for the sick, poor, those who are weak. And finally, the little finger is the smallest. That's you. Pray for your needs and wants. God already knows all our needs and wants before we come to Him, but He loves us to come to Him and tell Him. He wants us to talk to Him and more importantly, to take time to be quiet and listen to what He is telling us. Below is a drawing of this. I also try to remember in each prayer to be thankful, give praise, confess and ask forgiveness, pray for others, and then myself.

But the fruit of the Spirit is love, joy, peace, patience, kindness, goodness, faithfulness, gentleness, self-control; against such things there is no law.

Galatians 5:22-23

Peace

Peace- A state of mutual harmony between people or groups.

Welcome to Day 3

Here are the verses for the day that all have the word peace in them. Continue your challenge of finding other verses. Choose one or more to share on our website (go to blog for Day 3- Peace).

 Hebrews 12:14 *"Follow peace with all men, and holiness, without which no man shall see the Lord."*

 James 3:18 *"And the fruit of righteousness is sown in peace of them that make peace."*

 **Philippians 4:7** *"And the peace of God which passeth all understanding shall keep your hearts and minds through Christ Jesus."*

Psalm 29:11 *"The LORD will give strength unto His people; the LORD will bless His people with peace."*

Psalm 34:14 *"Depart from evil and do good; seek peace and pursue it."*

Isaiah 26:3 *"Thou wilt keep him in perfect peace, whose mind is stayed on Thee: because he trusteth in Thee."*

John 16:33 *"These things I have spoken unto you, that in Me ye might have peace. In the world, ye shall have tribulation: but be of good cheer; I have overcome the world."*

John 14:27 *"Peace I leave with you, my peace I give unto you; not as the world giveth, give I unto you. Let not your heart be troubled, neither let it be afraid."*

Romans 15:13 *"Now the God of hope will fill you with all joy and peace in believing, that ye may abound in hope, through the power of the Holy Ghost."*

Have you ever sat on a rock beside a stream and just listened to the trickling water?

How about climbed a mountain or hill where you could look out and see God's wonderful creation below?

Have you prayed for something and then listened for God's voice to touch your Spirit?

To me, these define peace—at least, peace of the soul. I know there are other kinds of peace: no war, disturbing the peace, keeping the peace, etc. But I like to think of peace as quiet, stillness, and harmony like some of the examples above.

For our activity today, I have a word search using the words in John 14:27. Hope you enjoy it.

Before you go to the next page for that, remember to pray and ask God to help you show the fruits of the Spirit in your daily life so that you are following His commands and being the example to others in the world. I would love to see your comments on our website on today's "fruit" or any that we have studied so far. We now have LOVE, JOY, and PEACE.

Peace John 14:27

```
Y C U B A R T M O D O F G N D
A T D Z N W K V L E T N X Y U
G G D L C D E F R S D Y M G V
X P K H P V R G I V E T H R D
K T D I Y T J G P D L R O W E
J I I O H Q Z K E C A E P V S
A T A L T H A L U S Z G A V J
T F R R S N B R Z S R E S H B
Y F F C P U U T B A L B H V L
Q Y A W O O J O E H T R L F H
U O P R Y I Y N E F Y H S L Z
V U T W Z Z A B S Y X A S Z
E V I G Y R R T G B C Z F B P
S T B Y E T L T V K J O K X Q
H T O Z J X R E H T I E N T I
```

PEACE   BE
LEAVE   TROUBLED
WITH   NEITHER
YOU   IT
MY   AFRAID
GIVE
NOT
AS
THE
WORLD
GIVETH
UNTO
LET
YOUR
HEART

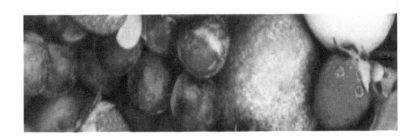

Patience

Patience- To be even-tempered, not easily angered, to be calm amidst conflict and turmoil.

Welcome to Day 4

Glad to have you back for day 4 of our study. Here are the verses containing patience. Continue your challenge to find more. Remember to post those on our website (go to blog for Day 4- Patience).

 Romans 12:12 *"Rejoicing in hope; patient in tribulation; continuing instant in prayer."*

 **Psalm 37:7** *"Rest in the LORD and wait patiently for Him: fret not thyself because of him who prospereth in his way, because of the man who bringeth wicked devices to pass."*

 **Psalm 40:1** *"I waited patiently for the LORD; and He inclined unto me and heard my cry."*

 **Romans 8:25** *"But if we hope for that we see not, then do we with* patience *wait for it."*

 Ecclesiastes 7:8 *"Better is the end of a thing than the beginning thereof: and the* patient *in spirit is better than the proud in spirit."*

 Romans 5:3-5 *"And not only so but we glory in tribulations also: knowing that tribulation worketh* patience*; and* patience*, experience; and experience, hope; and hope maketh not ashamed because the love of God is shed abroad in our hearts by the Holy Ghost which is given unto us."*

 **Hebrews 10:36** *"For ye have need of* patience*, that, after all ye have done the will of God, ye might receive the promise."*

 James 1:4 *"But let* patience *have her perfect work, that ye may be perfect and enter, wanting nothing."*

James 5:8 *"Be ye also patient; stablish your hearts: for the coming of the Lord draweth night."*

Oh my, I lacked patience as a young person. My mom called me "a little spitfire." She was the epitome of patient, but I didn't get that gene. As I got older, I realized that I needed to learn to be patient, so I prayed for it and gradually learned it fairly well. But a little of that spitfire is way down deep and will sometimes erupt if I do not let God lead me.

When I was a schoolteacher, many people said I had the patience of Job. That was only because God called me for that purpose and helped me see better ways like encouragement and praise to help students become the best they could be. I miss those days.

And speaking of Job, I don't believe he had patience as much as an unbelievable faith and trust in God. If you're not familiar with his story, be sure to take time to read it today.

For our closing activity today, find as many words as you can from the word PATIENCE. Words must be at least 2 letters. No letter can be repeated more times than it appears (only e can be used twice). Oh, and set the timer for 2 minutes. And go!

PATIENCE

Boggle anyone!!! I will post my 50 words that I found on the website blog page for day 4.

Kindness

Kindness- To be mild, gentle, humane, benevolent

Welcome to Day 5

Hope you're ready for day 5. We're half-way through our "fruits." Here are the verses today that contain kindness. Remember to continue your challenge of finding more and posting them on the website (go to blog for Day 5- Kindness).

 Ephesians 4:32 *"And be ye kind one to another, tenderhearted, forgiving one another, even as God for Christ's sake hath forgiven you".*

 **Psalm 17:7** *"Shew thy marvelous lovingkindness, O Thou that savest by Thy right hand them which put their trust in Thee from those that rise up against them."*

 **Psalm 31:21** *"Blessed be the LORD; for He hath shewed me His marvelous kindness in a strong city."*

Psalm 117:2 *"For His merciful kindness is great toward us: and the truth of the LORD endureth forever. Praise ye the LORD."*

Proverbs 19:22 *"The desire of a man is his kindness: and a poor man is better than a liar."*

Luke 6:35b *"For he is kind unto the unthankful and to the evil."*

Romans 12:10 *"Be kindly affectioned one to another with brotherly love; in honor preferring one another."*

1 Corinthians 13:4 *"Charity suffereth long and is kind; charity envieth not; charity vaunteth not itself; is not puffed up."*

Psalm 36:7 *"How excellent is thy lovingkindness, O God: therefore the children of men put their trust under the shadow of thy wings."*

Kindness. Oh, to have more of this in the world today. We are in the midst of the coronavirus in 2020 as I write this. You would think people would stop and take a look at their lives and what they are doing to cause God to be so angry with His creation. Instead of being kind and helping each other, some people are rushing out and hoarding basic supplies so that people, especially the elderly and poor, are unable to have their basic needs met. That is one reason the world needed a wake-up call. But if they don't take this time to kneel before God and ask forgiveness and turn back to Him, He may not give us another opportunity. That doesn't mean everyone is acting this way. I have loved seeing the stories of people feeding the truckers, making masks for the medical teams, providing on-line worship services so Christians can continue to hear God's Word, and many neighborhoods providing for the elderly, shut-ins, sick, or those with children to care for because schools are closed for this academic year. I am thankful for our education staff in doing distance learning and feeding those in need. A special thank you and continuing prayer to our leaders and all those trying to help us through this pandemic. Even now, the Trump haters won't let up. Whether they are your choice or not, remember that we are told to pray for them. Check out Romans 13:1 (NIV) *"Let everyone be subject to the governing authorities, for there is no authority except that which God has established".* The authorities that exist have been established by God. Our president, senators, governors, mayors, etc. are placed there under God's authority. So, whether they were your choice or not, show respect. Keep the negativity to yourself and let our nation heal. In other words, BE KIND!!!

Before you end your study today, pray for our country, our leaders, and to fill your heart with kindness. Let's grab that promise of healing in our land when we all agree together and work toward this goal. (2 Chronicles 7:14)

For our closing activity, fill in the blanks of this verse. Psalm 36:7

How _____ is Thy _____

O God: therefore the _____ of

_____ put their _____

under the _____ ____ _____

_____.

Goodness

Goodness- Virtuous, morally excellent, righteous

Welcome to Day 6

Our time is going so fast. We are two-thirds of the way finished with our "fruits." Here are the verses for today that contain goodness. Remember to find some of your own and post them on our website (go to blog for Day 6- Goodness).

 Romans 12:21 *"Be not overcome of evil but overcome evil with good."*

 Nahum 1:7 *"The LORD is good, a stronghold in the day of trouble; and He knoweth them that trust in Him."*

 **Psalm 37:3** *"Trust in the LORD and do good; so shalt thou dwell in the land, and verily thou shalt be fed."*

 **James 1:17** *"Every good gift and every perfect gift is from above, and cometh down from the Father of lights, with whom is no variableness, neither shadow of turning."*

 **Romans 8:28** *"And we know that all things work together for good to them that love God, to them who are the called according to His purpose."*

 Mark 10:18 *"And Jesus said unto him, Why callest thou me good? There is none good but one, that is, God."*

 Psalm 26:3 *"Surely goodness and mercy shall follow me all the days of my life: and I will dwell in the house of the LORD forever."*

 **Psalm 31:19** *"Oh how great is thy goodness, which Thou hast laid up for them that fear Thee; which Thou hast wrought for them that trust in Thee before the sons of men."*

Psalm 144:2 *"My goodness and my fortress; my high tower, and my deliverer; my shield and He in whom I trust; who subdueth my people under me."*

Do you remember in Sunday School as a child singing the chorus: God is so good, God is so good, God is so good, He's so good to me.

I challenge you to take a few minutes to lift up a prayer thanking God for His goodness. List all those things that are good in your life. Be careful not to let Satan enter those thoughts with negatives because he will do all he can to make that happen.

In Acts, we learn of a good man and what that meant. Barnabas loved God and others according to Luke. These two loves are the great commandment. Barnabas walked by faith and in the Holy Spirit. No one is truly good but if we strive to follow the examples of Barnabas, we can do our best. First, you have to accept Jesus as your Savior knowing He is the Son of God, that He died for our sins to be forgiven, and that He arose to be our intercessor at the throne of God. Only then can we love God and others, walk by faith, and have the Holy Spirit dwell in us. Reading God's Word daily help us grow closer to Him and understand His Words to live by. Don't forget after reading to give time in quiet to LISTEN to God speak to you.

Hope you've felt GOOD about the lesson today.

For our closing activity, let's do another acrostic poem using the word GOODNESS. Be sure and post yours on website (go to blog for Day 6- Goodness).

G

O

O

D

N

E

S

S

Here's my acrostic for today.

God's love and mercy given every day
Our home He provided for a place to stay
Others include our friends and family
Desires we have and daily provides for our needs
Never leaves us when we call to Him in prayer
Earth to live on until He calls us in the air
Seasons and sunsets and sunshine too
Salvation He gives to me and to you

Faithfulness

Faith- The substance of things hoped for, the evidence of things not seen.

Welcome to Day 7

Here we are on day 7. This is going too fast. Hope you're enjoying the "fruits" and will be applying them to your daily walk with the Lord. Here are our verses today that contain faithfulness. Remember to look for more and post those on our website (go to blog for Day 7- Faithfulness).

1 Corinthians 4:2 *"Moreover, it is required in stewards that a man be found faithful."*

1 John 1:9 *"If we confess our sins, He is faithful and just to forgive us our sins, and to cleanse us from all unrighteousness."*

Matthew 25:21 *"His lord said unto him, Well done, thou good and faithful servant: thou hast been faithful over a few things; I will make thee ruler over many things: enter thou into the joy of thy lord."*

1 Corinthians 1:9 *"God is faithful, by whom ye were called unto the fellowship of his Son Jesus Christ our Lord."*

2 Thessalonians 3:3 *"But the Lord is faithful, who shall stablish you, and keep you from evil."*

Proverbs 28:20 *"A faithful man shall abound with blessings: but he that maketh haste to be rich shall not be innocent."*

Deuteronomy 7:9 *"Know therefore that the LORD thy God, He is God, the faithful God, which keepeth covenant and mercy with them that love Him and keep His commandments to a thousand generations.*

Psalm 36:5 *"Thy mercy, O LORD, is in the heavens; and Thy faithfulness reachest unto the clouds."*

 **Psalm 143:1** *"Hear my prayer, O LORD, give ear to my supplications: in Thy faithfulness, answer me, and in Thy righteousness."*

When I think of people in the Bible that showed great faith, a few come to mind:
1. Abraham being asked to sacrifice his son, Isaac.
2. Elijah challenging the prophets of Baal.
3. Moses leading the Israelites away from Egyptian slavery.

There are many others. I think my favorite one is of Daniel. He showed great faith from the time he was captured and trained for service in Babylon, reading the handwriting on the wall, and interpreting the dreams of the king. But my most favorite is the story of him being thrown in the lion's den because he would not stop praying to God as he always had before. That was great faith. He even made a believer out of the king who couldn't believe it when he found Daniel alive the next morning.

Many songs have been written about faith: *Great is Thy Faithfulness, Have Faith in God, and Faith is the Victory* are a few of the old hymns. Some new contemporary worship songs are *Walk by Faith* by Jeremy Camp, *By Faith* by Keith & Kristyn Getty, and *Let Faith Arise* by Bridge City.

For our closing activity today, choose a song above or one of your own about Faith and write the lyrics. Here is my pick: *Let Faith Arise* by Bridge City

Knock; and the doors will open.
Speak; and the mountains will move.
Anything we ask God, God can do.
Believe in the One who freed us.
Trust in the One who hears us.
'Cause anything we ask God, God can do.
Chorus: Let faith arise, let faith arise.
            God is on our side. God is on our side.
            We'll overcome, the battle's won.
            Our Savior King, our victory.
Bridge: God is with us, He is for us.
            Faithful is our God.

Don't you love how these songs are ripped right from the scriptures. I do. Well, don't forget to post to the website on the blog for day 7. See you tomorrow.

Gentleness

Gentle- meek, sensitive, kindness of behavior, calm, to pacify

Welcome to Day 8

Day 8. Only one day left after today. I hope you have enjoyed learning the "fruits" of the Spirit and will let them lead you daily in your walk. Here are our verses for today that contain gentleness. Remember to find some of your own and post them on our website (go to blog for Day 8- Gentleness).

 2 Samuel 22:36 *"Thou hast also given me the shield of salvation: and thy gentleness hath made me great."*

 Psalm 18:35 *"Thou hast also given me the shield of salvation: and thy right hand hath holden me up, and thy gentleness hath made me great."*

2 Timothy 2:24 *"And the servant of the Lord must not strive but be gentle unto all men, apt to teach, patient."*

James 3:17 *"But the wisdom that is from above is first pure, then peaceable, gentle, and easy to be entreated, full of mercy and good fruits, without partiality and without hypocrisy."*

Titus 3:1-2 *"Put them in mind to be subject to principalities and powers, to obey magistrates, to be ready to every good work, to speak evil of no man, to be no brawlers, but gentle, shewing all meekness unto all men."*

1 Peter 2:18 *Servants, be subject to your masters with all fear; not only to the good and gentle, but also to the froward."*

Isaiah 40:11 *"He shall feed his flock like a shepherd: He shall gather the lambs with his arm and carry them in His bosom and shall gently lead those that are with young."*

Zephaniah 2:3 *"Seek ye the LORD, all ye meek of the earth, which have wrought His judgement; see righteousness, see meekness: it may be ye shall be hid in the day of the LORD's anger."*

1 Corinthians 4:21 *"What will ye? Shall I come unto you with a rod or in love, and in a spirit of meekness?*

When I think of the word gentle, I think of a lamb. Maybe that's because of the most gentle of all- the Lamb of God.

The Greek word for gentle is praus [πραΰς]. It is synonymous with meek and used in several verses of the Bible. It is defined as: not being overly impressed by a sense of one's self-importance. That describes Jesus. He humbled Himself to leave

His throne to come to earth to be the Savior of all mankind that believed He was the Son of God, died for us all, and rose the third day to live in heaven and become our interceder to God's throne of mercy and grace.

In one concordance, Jesus was described as gentle or meek in 17 different verses. These were verses where Jesus was called the Lamb of God. One of my favorites if John 1:29 *"Behold! The Lamb of God which taketh away the sin of the world."* Now that's some great news!!! We are all sinners but can be washed as white as snow if we come to Jesus, confess, and accept Him as Lord and Savior of our life. Our lives should look different when that happens. Stay in God's Word daily, pray continually, and follow the commands given to us.

I'm sharing a hymn today written by Bill and Gloria Gaither. I loved to watch the Gaither Gospel Hour and was fortunate to get to see them perform in Bristol on their tour. I hope you enjoy this old hymn, *Gentle Shepherd.*
Gentle Shepherd, come and lead us. For we need You to help us find our way. Gentle Shepherd, come and feed us. For we need Your strength from day to day. There's no other we can turn to who can help us face another day.

Gentle Shepherd, come and lead us. For we need to you to help us find our way.

Does this not describe Jesus perfectly? He is and always will be our gentle Shepherd.

For our closing activity today, solve this code based on the verse 2 Samuel 22:36b.

A=@ D=% E=3 G=& H=^ L=!
M=~ N=# R=} S=$ T=+ Y=*

___ ___ ___
 +   ^   *

___ ___ ___ ___ ___ ___ ___ ___ ___ ___
 &   3   #   +   !   3   #   3 $ $

___ ___ ___ ___   ___ ___ ___ ___
 ^   @   +   ^   ~   @   %   3

___ ___   ___ ___ ___ ___ ___.
 ~   3   &   }   3   @   +

Self-Control

Self-control- Restraint and control over your actions, feelings, etc.

Welcome to Day 9

I don't know about you, but I cannot believe how quickly these days have gone by. Here is our last "fruit" to go over with the verses about self-control. You will see other words used that mean the same as self-control. Remember to continue your challenge of finding more and posting them on the website (go to blog for Day 9- Self control).

 **James 1:19-20** *"Wherefore my beloved brethren, let every man be swift to hear, slow to speak, slow to wrath: for the wrath of man worketh not the righteousness of God."*

 2 Peter 1:5-7 *"And beside this, giving all diligence, add to your faith virtue; and to virtue knowledge; and to knowledge temperance; and to temperance patience; and to patience godliness;*

and to godliness brotherly kindness; and to brotherly kindness charity."

Ephesians 6:11 *"Put on the whole armor of God that ye may be able to stand against the wiles of the devil."*

Romans 12:2 *"And be not conformed to this world; but be ye transformed by the renewing of your mind, that ye may prove what is that good and acceptable, and perfect will of God."*

Proverbs 16:32 *"He that is slow to anger is better than the mighty; and he that ruleth his spirit than he that taketh a city."*

Proverbs 25:28 *"He that hath no rule over his own spirit is like a city that is broken down and without walls."*

Titus 2:11-12 *"For the grace of God that bringeth salvation hath appeared to all men, teaching us that, denying ungodliness and worldly lusts, we should live soberly, righteously, and godly in this present world."*

 **Matthew 6:13** *"And lead us not into* temptation *but deliver us from evil. For Thine is the kingdom and the power and the glory forever. Amen."*

 **James 1:12** *"Blessed is the man that endureth* temptation*: for when he is tried, he shall receive the crown of life which the Lord hath promised to them that* love *Him."*

I think of King David when I think of self-control. He didn't have it when he had an affair with a married woman and killed her husband to have her. But after he asked God to forgive him, he learned it. When he was a young boy, he played the harp for King Saul. He killed Goliath in a battle and the people started singing his praises. This made King Saul really jealous. Even so much that he threw his spear at David trying to kill him as he played the harp for him. Did King Saul have self-control? I think not!!! King Saul continued to chase after David when David escaped the palace. King Saul and his army stopped to take a break from chasing David and his men. King Saul went into a cave where David and his men were hiding. David's men urged him to kill King Saul. David refused saying that Saul was the anointed ruler of God. If you don't know how the story ends, you need to read 1 & 2 Samuel.

I wish people in our nation could act like David and realize that whoever is in authority has been allowed to be there by God. Our nation needs to learn respect and honor again so that God will heal our land. Please be in prayer for this.

As you end this lesson, offer up your prayer to God asking that He heal our land. I would love to see revival all over the world with people coming to know Jesus as their Savior and living like they know it is true.

For our closing activity, using the letters in SELF-CONTROL, list things you can do to practice self-control in your life.

S E L F C O N T R O L

Here is my example of ways to show self-control. Be sure to post yours on the website (go to blog for day 9- self control). I really look forward to you sharing each day.

Silence

Exercise or a good walk

Leave the situation

Find a quiet place

Count to ten (or a hundred)

Open your Bible and read

Never let the heat of a moment catch you off guard

Try to avoid triggers

Relax or remove the temptation

Openly pray

Listen to God's still small voice instead of the
        raging one in your head

But the fruit of the Spirit is love, joy, peace, patience, kindness, goodness, faithfulness, gentleness, self-control; against such things there is no law. Galatians 5:22-23 ESV

photo courtesy of Life323.com

Closing Remarks

I cannot believe we have come to the end of our study. I hope these past few days have brought you closer to the Lord as you've studied the ways our character should be if we are a believer.

I hope your study of God's Word continues after this time learning the fruits of the Spirit.

I am leaving today open for your comments, prayers, and anything you would like to share. Even when the study has ended, the website will still be open for you. Please feel free to go there often and share. I will continue to monitor the page and I hope those that follow it will as well.

Remember to have the fruits of the Spirit pouring from you daily: love, joy, peace, patience, kindness, goodness, faithfulness, gentleness, and self-control. Are they rolling off your tongue yet? Go back to the introduction page and listen to the song again. That'll help you learn them.

For the final activity of this study, I created a SUDOKU puzzle for the fruits. 9 fruits = perfect

SUDOKU. To make it easier to fill in the boxes, use this code:
L=love J=joy Pe=peace Pa=patience K=kindness
Go=goodness F=faithfulness Ge=gentleness
S=self-control

Just as in number Sudoku, each row, column, and box must contain each of the 9 fruits. Good luck and have fun. Thanks for joining me on this journey. I hope you have enjoyed it.

Fruits of the Spirit Sudoku

Ge				F	Go	Pe		
Pe	F	L	Ge			Pa		
S	K					Ge		F
		J		Pe		K	Ge	L
L		K				Go		Pe
	Pe	Ge	K	Go	L			
Go			Pa	Ge			Pe	
	Ge	S			Pe	L		Go
K		Pe		L		F		

But the fruit of the Spirit is LOVE, JOY, PEACE, PATIENCE, KINDNESS, GOODNESS, FAITHFULNESS, GENTLENESS, AND SELF-CONTROL. Against such things there is no law.

Galatians 5:22-23

About the Author

Victoria Fletcher has attended the First Baptist Church in Damascus, Virginia, since she was born. She jokes that she was there before because her mother attended there, too. She worked with the children for 43 years in Sunday School, Children's Choir, and Vacation Bible School.

She was a schoolteacher for the Washington County Schools for 30 years. Then she became the secretary/ministry assistant at her church for 8 years. Now she is the owner and operator of Hoot Books Publishing that prepares books for publishing for herself and other authors. Her office is currently located at the Virginia Highlands Small Business Incubator in Abingdon, Virginia.

She has always loved taking part in Bible studies. This is her first attempt at writing one. She also enjoys writing children's books, devotionals, poetry, and a few other genres thrown in there. You can see her books at victoriafletcher.biz.

Please feel free to contact her at: vfletcher56@gmail.com or on her Facebook pages: Victoria Fletcher's Books, Hoot Books Publishing, and the one for this study, Fruits of the Spirit. Sorry, the link is not ready until the page goes Live but if you search for Fruits of the Spirit, look for this logo—

The Fruit of the spirit